MODERN MACHIAVELLI

Outfox Them All: Machiavelli's Lessons for Modern Success

Marlon Gladstone

Novel Notions Publishing

The characters and events portrayed in this book are fictitious. Any similarity to real persons, living or dead, is coincidental and not intended by the author.

ISBN 978-1-926481-18-0

INTRODUCTION:

Machiavelli's Enduring Wisdom in the Modern World

In the annals of political philosophy, few works have stirred as much controversy, admiration, and continued relevance as Niccolò Machiavelli's "The Prince." Written in 1513, this slim volume has cast a long shadow over the centuries, influencing leaders, thinkers, and strategists across diverse fields. Today, in our rapidly evolving, globally connected world, one might wonder: What can a Renaissance-era treatise on statecraft teach us about navigating the complexities of modern business, politics, and personal success?

The answer, perhaps surprisingly, is a great deal. Machiavelli's insights into human nature, power dynamics, and strategic thinking are not relics of a bygone era but timeless principles that can provide a significant advantage to those who understand and apply them in contemporary contexts. This book aims to bridge the gap between Machiavelli's 16th-century wisdom and the challenges of the 21st century, offering readers a powerful toolkit for success in today's competitive landscape.

Machiavelli wrote "The Prince" during a time of great turmoil in Italy. The peninsula was fragmented into numerous small states, vulnerable to invasion by more powerful neighbors and wracked by internal conflicts. This environment of constant change, fierce competition, and existential threats bears striking similarities to our modern business world, where disruption is the norm, and only the most adaptable survive.

By delving into Machiavelli's principles and reinterpreting them for our time, we can gain several key advantages:

1. Strategic Thinking

Machiavelli's approach to strategy is fundamentally about understanding the reality of a situation, free from moral or idealistic blinders. In business, this translates to a clear-eyed assessment of market conditions, competitor strengths and weaknesses, and one's own capabilities. By adopting this ruthlessly pragmatic mindset, modern leaders can make more effective decisions, unencumbered by wishful thinking or outdated assumptions.

For instance, Machiavelli's advice to princes about the importance of adapting to changing circumstances is particularly relevant in today's fast-paced business environment. Companies that cling to outdated business models or fail to innovate quickly find themselves obsolete. The fall of Kodak, once a giant in the photography industry, serves as a cautionary tale of what happens when a company fails to adapt to technological changes.

2. Understanding Power Dynamics

One of Machiavelli's key contributions was his analysis of power: how it is gained, maintained, and lost. In the corporate world, understanding these dynamics can be crucial for navigating office politics, negotiating deals, or leading teams. Machiavelli's insights can help you recognize the true power structures within an organization, beyond the official hierarchy, and operate more effectively within them.

Consider, for example, Machiavelli's advice about the importance of appearing virtuous while being prepared to act otherwise when necessary. In a modern context, this might translate to maintaining a positive public image and strong company culture, while also being prepared to make tough decisions for the sake of the business. Companies like Amazon have faced criticism for their hard-driving culture, but this approach has also contributed to their remarkable success.

3. Risk Management

Machiavelli lived in uncertain times, and much of "The Prince" is devoted to managing risk and uncertainty. His concept of "fortuna" (fortune or luck) and how it interacts with individual agency ("virtù") offers a sophisticated framework for thinking about risk in business and life.

In today's volatile global economy, the ability to assess and manage risk is more critical than ever. Machiavelli's teachings can help leaders develop resilience, create contingency plans, and seize opportunities when they arise. The success of companies like Netflix, which took the bold risk of pivoting from DVD rentals to streaming, exemplifies the Machiavellian principle of adapting to changing fortunes.

4. Leadership Skills

While some of Machiavelli's advice may seem harsh by modern standards, his fundamental insights into leadership remain relevant. He understood that effective leadership requires a combination of strength and flexibility, the ability to inspire loyalty, and the wisdom to surround oneself with capable advisors.

Modern leaders who study Machiavelli can learn valuable lessons about building and maintaining authority, motivating teams, and making difficult decisions. For instance, Machiavelli's advice about the importance of appearing merciful while being prepared to act decisively against threats is mirrored in the "tough but fair" leadership style often praised in successful CEOs.

5. Competitive Advantage

In a world where information is readily available and competitive advantages are quickly eroded, the insights gained from Machiavelli can provide a unique edge. By understanding the deeper principles of strategy and power dynamics, you can operate on a different level than competitors who are merely reacting to surface-level trends.

For example, Machiavelli's advice about the importance of understanding the desires and motivations of others can be applied to modern marketing and customer relationship management. Companies that truly understand their customers' needs and pain points, rather than just reacting to superficial preferences, can create more compelling products and build stronger brand loyalty.

6. Ethical Navigation

While Machiavelli is often associated with amoral or even immoral behavior, a careful reading of his work reveals a more nuanced perspective. He was writing for leaders who had to make difficult decisions in a harsh world. By grappling with Machiavelli's ideas, modern readers can develop a more sophisticated understanding of ethical dilemmas in business and politics.

This doesn't mean adopting an "anything goes" mentality, but rather developing the ability to navigate complex ethical terrain where the right course of action isn't always clear. In an era where businesses are increasingly expected to balance profit with social responsibility, this nuanced ethical thinking is more valuable than ever.

7. Personal Empowerment

Perhaps most importantly, Machiavelli's teachings offer a path to personal empowerment. By understanding the principles that govern power dynamics and strategic success, individuals can take more control over their own destinies. Whether you're climbing the corporate ladder, starting a business, or pursuing any ambitious goal, Machiavellian thinking can help you navigate obstacles and seize opportunities.

It's important to note that embracing Machiavelli's principles doesn't mean becoming cynical or abandoning one's values. Rather, it means developing a clearer understanding of how the world works and how to operate effectively within it. It's about being pragmatic and strategic in pursuit of your goals, while still maintaining your core ethical standards.

As we embark on this exploration of Machiavelli's ideas and their modern applications, it's worth remembering that knowledge is power. The principles you'll encounter in this book have been studied and applied by leaders and strategists for centuries. By adding these tools to your mental toolkit, you're equipping yourself to navigate the complexities of the modern world more effectively.

In the chapters that follow, we'll dive deep into Machiavelli's key concepts, examining how they can be applied in various aspects of modern life. We'll look at real-world examples of Machiavellian principles in action, both in business and beyond. We'll also address the ethical considerations of applying these ideas, helping you strike a balance between effectiveness and integrity.

Whether you're a business leader looking to gain a competitive edge, a professional aiming to advance your career, or simply someone interested in understanding the dynamics of power and success, this book offers valuable insights. By the time you finish, you'll have a new perspective on how to approach challenges, seize opportunities, and achieve your goals in our complex, fast-paced world.

Machiavelli wrote that "a wise man ought always to follow the paths beaten by great men, and to imitate those who have been supreme." In studying Machiavelli himself – one of history's most influential political thinkers – we have the opportunity to gain insights that have guided leaders for generations. Let us now embark on this journey of discovery, as we uncover the timeless wisdom of Machiavelli and learn how to apply it in our modern lives.

CHAPTER I:

The Prince's First Lesson for Modern Leaders

In the tumultuous world of 16th-century Italy, Niccolò Machiavelli penned "The Prince," a guidebook for rulers that has echoed through the centuries. While Machiavelli wrote for princes and potentates, his insights are surprisingly relevant in today's corporate landscape. Let's dive into his first principle - the types of principalities - and see how it translates to our modern business world.

The Old and the New: Machiavelli's Principalities

Machiavelli kicked off "The Prince" by categorizing states into two main types: hereditary principalities and new principalities. Hereditary principalities were those passed down through family lines, while new principalities were freshly acquired territories. He further divided new principalities into those acquired by one's own arms and virtue, by fortune and foreign arms, or by wickedness.

Now, you might be thinking, "What does this have to do with my company or career?" Well, more than you might expect. Let's break it down and see how Machiavelli's 500-year-old ideas still pack a punch in today's business world.

Hereditary Principalities: The Family Business

In Machiavelli's time, hereditary principalities were territories ruled by the same family for generations. The Prince of such a state had the advantage of established traditions and loyal subjects, making his rule generally more stable.

Fast forward to today, and we see a similar dynamic in family-owned businesses. These companies, passed down through generations, often enjoy a strong reputation, loyal customer base, and deep-rooted company culture. Think of companies like Walmart, still controlled by the Walton family, or Ford Motor Company, which has had a member of the Ford family in leadership for over a century.

However, just as Machiavelli warned princes not to become complacent, family businesses face unique challenges. They must innovate to stay relevant while respecting their heritage. The modern "prince" of a family business must balance tradition with progress, much like Machiavelli's hereditary ruler had to maintain stability while adapting to new threats.

Take the case of Lego, the Danish toy company. Founded in 1932 by Ole Kirk Kristiansen, it remained in family hands but faced near-bankruptcy in the early 2000s. The company's turnaround came when they embraced innovation, expanding into digital products and popular branded sets, while staying true to their core product. This balance of tradition and innovation is a perfect example of how a "hereditary principality" can thrive in the modern era.

New Principalities: The Startup Scene

Now, let's turn to what Machiavelli called "new principalities." In today's terms, think startups, new ventures, or newly acquired businesses. Machiavelli divided these into three categories, each with a modern equivalent.

1. Acquired by One's Own Arms and Virtue: The Self-Made Entrepreneur

Machiavelli believed that principalities acquired through one's own skill and effort were the most admirable and secure. In today's world, this translates to the self-made entrepreneur, the startup founder who builds a company from scratch.

Consider Jeff Bezos and Amazon. Starting from a garage in Seattle, Bezos built Amazon into one of the world's most valuable companies. Like Machiavelli's ideal prince, Bezos relied on his own "arms and virtue" - his vision, strategic thinking, and relentless drive for innovation.

Another example is Sara Blakely, who turned $5,000 and a brilliant idea into Spanx, a billion-dollar shapewear company. Blakely's journey embodies Machiavelli's concept of using one's own arms and virtue to build a "new principality."

However, Machiavelli warned that these new states are the most difficult to establish. This rings true in the startup world, where the failure rate is notoriously high. The modern entrepreneur, like Machiavelli's prince, must overcome skepticism, establish new systems, and win loyalty in a competitive landscape.

2. Acquired by Fortune: The Lucky Break

Machiavelli next discussed principalities acquired through good fortune or the arms of others. He argued that while these were easy to acquire, they were challenging to maintain.

In the business world, this might translate to companies that achieve sudden success through a stroke of luck, or businesses inherited or gifted rather than built from the ground up. While it might seem like hitting the jackpot, managing such sudden success can be tricky.

Consider the case of Minecraft creator Markus Persson. He created a wildly successful game almost by accident, leading to a $2.5 billion buyout from Microsoft. However, Persson struggled with the sudden wealth and fame, eventually selling the company and stepping away from game development.

Another example is the story of MySpace. Once the king of social media, it was acquired by News Corporation for $580 million in 2005. However, unable to maintain its position against rising competitors like Facebook, MySpace's value plummeted. This illustrates Machiavelli's point that fortunes gained easily are often the hardest to maintain.

For the modern leader who finds themselves in a position of sudden success or inheriting a thriving business, Machiavelli's advice would be to quickly establish a strong foundation. This means understanding the source of the company's success, building strong teams, and being prepared to face challenges that the original founder may have navigated instinctively.

3. Acquired by Wickedness: The Hostile Takeover

Machiavelli's final category of new principalities were those acquired through wicked or unethical means. While he didn't endorse such methods, he analyzed them dispassionately, noting that they can be effective if the cruelty is applied swiftly and not repeated.

In the modern business world, this might translate to hostile takeovers or businesses built through unethical practices. While we certainly can't endorse unethical behavior, we can learn from Machiavelli's analysis of its effects.

Consider the case of Uber under its co-founder and former CEO, Travis Kalanick. Uber's aggressive expansion tactics, including flouting local regulations and fostering a cutthroat company culture, initially drove rapid growth. However, the accumulation of scandals eventually led to Kalanick's ouster and a major company overhaul.

Another example is the hostile takeover of Anheuser-Busch by InBev in 2008. InBev's aggressive tactics were successful in acquiring the iconic American brewer, but led to significant cultural clashes and reputational challenges in the aftermath.

Machiavelli's insight here is particularly relevant: actions perceived as wicked or unethical might bring short-term gains, but they often lead to long-term instability. In today's world of social media and instant communication, unethical business practices are more likely than ever to come to light and damage a company's reputation.

The Modern Prince: Navigating Today's Business

Landscape

So, how can today's business leaders apply Machiavelli's insights on principalities to their work? Here are a few key takeaways:

1. Understand Your Foundation

Whether you're leading a long-established family business or a fresh startup, understand the nature of your "principality." Each type comes with its own strengths and challenges.

For family businesses, leverage your heritage and loyal customer base, but don't let tradition stifle innovation. For startups, your agility and fresh perspective are assets, but you'll need to work hard to establish credibility and systems.

2. Be Prepared for Challenges

Machiavelli warned that new principalities face the most difficulties. In the business world, this translates to the high failure rate of new ventures. If you're leading a startup or a newly acquired business, be prepared for challenges and resistance. Your vision and determination - your "virtue," in Machiavelli's terms - will be crucial.

3. Don't Rest on Your Laurels

For those who achieve success through a stroke of luck or inherit a successful business, remember Machiavelli's warning: these "principalities" are often the hardest to maintain. Don't take your success for granted. Work quickly to understand the sources of the company's success and establish your own strong foundation.

4. Ethics Matter

While Machiavelli is often accused of advocating for unethical behavior, a careful reading shows he understood the long-term instability it causes. In today's interconnected world, unethical business practices are more likely than ever to be exposed and punished. Build your business on a foundation of integrity for long-term success.

5. Adapt to Your Environment

Machiavelli emphasized the importance of understanding and adapting to one's environment. In today's rapidly changing business landscape, this advice is more relevant than ever. Stay attuned to market trends, technological advancements, and shifts in consumer behavior. The modern "prince" must be agile and ready to pivot when necessary.

6. Build Strong Relationships

Whether you're leading an established company or a new venture, strong relationships are crucial. Machiavelli spoke of the importance of having the support of either the nobles or the common people. In business terms, this translates to building strong relationships with your team, customers, investors, and other stakeholders.

7. Continuous Learning

Machiavelli's "The Prince" was essentially a guide for continuous learning and improvement in leadership. Today's business leaders should adopt the same mindset. The business world is constantly evolving, and the most successful leaders are those who never stop learning and adapting.

Conclusion: The Timeless Wisdom of Machiavelli

Machiavelli's analysis of principalities, written five centuries ago for the rulers of Italian city-states, still offers valuable insights for today's business leaders. Whether you're at the helm of a family-owned company with a century of history, a startup founder working from your garage, or a CEO who stumbled into unexpected success, Machiavelli's principles can help you navigate your path.

The key is to understand the nature of your "principality" - your business - and the unique challenges and opportunities it presents. By doing so, you can lead with the wisdom of a Renaissance prince and the innovation of a modern entrepreneur.

Remember, Machiavelli's prince wasn't just a ruler, but a student of power, politics, and human nature. In the same way, the modern business leader should be a perpetual student - of markets, of technology, of people, and of themselves.

So, the next time you're faced with a tough business decision, take a moment to consider: What would Machiavelli advise? You might find that this Renaissance thinker has more to offer the boardroom than you ever imagined.

CHAPTER II:

The Family Legacy: Machiavelli's Hereditary Principalities in Today's Business World

In "The Prince," Machiavelli argued that hereditary principalities were easier to maintain than newly acquired ones. The prince of a hereditary state, he reasoned, would face fewer difficulties as long as he didn't deviate too far from his ancestors' policies and adapted to unforeseen circumstances. This concept finds a striking parallel in today's world of family businesses and long-established corporations. Let's delve into how Machiavelli's insights on hereditary rule translate to modern business leadership.

The Stability of Tradition

Machiavelli believed that hereditary princes had a significant advantage: tradition. The people were accustomed to the ruling family, and this familiarity bred loyalty and stability. In the business world, we see this principle at work in successful family-owned companies and long-standing corporations.

Consider the case of Beretta, the oldest active manufacturer of firearm components in the world. Founded in 1526, Beretta has been owned by the same family for nearly 500 years. The company's longevity can be attributed, in part, to the stability that comes from consistent family leadership. Customers trust the Beretta name, and this trust has been built over generations.

Similarly, companies like Ford Motor Company, which has had a member of the Ford family in leadership roles since its founding in 1903, benefit from this sense of continuity. The Ford name carries weight with consumers and employees alike, providing a stable foundation for the company's operations.

The Challenge of Complacency

However, Machiavelli warned that hereditary princes shouldn't become complacent. While their position might be more secure, they still needed to adapt to changing circumstances. This advice rings especially true in today's fast-paced business environment.

Kodak serves as a cautionary tale in this regard. Once a dominant force in the photography industry, Kodak failed to adapt to the digital revolution, despite inventing the first digital camera. The company's long history and success in film photography led to a form of institutional inertia, ultimately resulting in bankruptcy in 2012.

On the flip side, we have companies like Nintendo, founded in 1889 as a playing card company. Nintendo has successfully navigated numerous technological shifts, evolving from playing cards to electronic games to become a leader in the video game industry. This ability to adapt while maintaining its core identity exemplifies Machiavelli's advice for hereditary rulers.

Balancing Tradition and Innovation

Machiavelli suggested that a hereditary prince should respect established customs while still being flexible enough to respond to new challenges. In the business world, this translates to maintaining core values and established practices while still embracing innovation and change.

The Marriott hotel chain provides an excellent example of this balance. Founded in 1927, Marriott has maintained a strong corporate culture based on its founder's values. However, the company has also been at the forefront of innovation in the hospitality industry, pioneering concepts like the airport hotel and continually adapting to changing consumer preferences.

Similarly, Japan's Kongo Gumi, the world's oldest continuously operating company until its acquisition in 2006, managed to stay in business for over 1,400 years by balancing tradition with adaptation. Founded in 578 AD, the construction company specialized in building Buddhist temples. While it maintained its core expertise, it also adapted to changing times, taking on new types of projects as Japan modernized.

The Power of Brand Legacy

Machiavelli noted that people are naturally inclined to favor their hereditary prince, all else being equal. In business terms, this translates to the power of brand legacy. Established companies often benefit from strong brand recognition and customer loyalty, which can be a significant competitive advantage.

Take, for example, luxury brands like Louis Vuitton or Hermès. These companies leverage their long histories and traditions of craftsmanship to command premium prices and maintain customer loyalty. The "hereditary" nature of their brand gives them an edge in a crowded marketplace.

However, as Machiavelli would caution, this advantage is not absolute. Newer companies can and do disrupt established markets. Tesla's rapid rise in the automotive industry, challenging century-old car manufacturers, is a prime example of how "new principalities" can successfully compete with "hereditary" ones.

The Responsibility of Stewardship

Machiavelli emphasized that a hereditary prince had a responsibility to maintain and enhance the state he inherited. In the business world, this translates to the concept of stewardship - the idea that leaders are temporary custodians of the company, responsible for passing it on in better shape than they found it.

The Tata Group in India exemplifies this principle. Founded in 1868, the company has been led by members of the Tata family for most of its history. However, the family views its role as stewards rather than owners, with a strong emphasis on ethical business practices and giving back to society. This approach has helped the company maintain public goodwill and navigate changing political and economic landscapes over more than 150 years.

Succession Planning: The Key to Longevity

While Machiavelli didn't explicitly discuss succession planning in his chapter on hereditary principalities, it's an essential consideration for modern "hereditary" businesses. The smooth transition of leadership is crucial for maintaining the stability that Machiavelli saw as the key advantage of hereditary rule.

Family businesses that fail to plan for succession often struggle or fail when the time comes to pass the baton. The Ambani brothers' feud over their father's Reliance Industries in India is a stark example of how succession issues can threaten even the most successful "hereditary" businesses.

On the other hand, companies like Walmart have managed successful transitions across generations. The Walton family has maintained control of the company while bringing in professional managers, ensuring both continuity and fresh perspectives.

Adapting to Modern Governance

While Machiavelli wrote about absolute monarchs, modern businesses operate in a world of shareholders, boards of directors, and regulatory oversight. "Hereditary" companies today must balance family or foundational control with good corporate governance.

Companies like Facebook (now Meta) and Google (Alphabet) have adopted dual-class share structures that allow their founders to maintain control while still being publicly traded. This modern adaptation of "hereditary" control has been both praised for allowing visionary leaders to pursue long-term strategies and criticized for reducing accountability.

Conclusion: The Enduring Wisdom of Machiavelli's Hereditary Principle

Machiavelli's insights on hereditary principalities offer valuable lessons for modern business leaders, particularly those in family businesses or long-established corporations. The advantages of tradition, brand legacy, and stability are significant, but they must be balanced with the need for innovation and adaptation.

The modern "hereditary prince" in business must navigate a complex landscape, maintaining the core values and practices that have led to long-term success while also being agile enough to respond to new challenges and opportunities. They must act as responsible stewards, planning for succession and adapting governance structures to modern requirements.

Ultimately, the success of a "hereditary" business in the modern world depends on its ability to honor its past while embracing the future. As Machiavelli might say if he were writing for today's business leaders: Respect your heritage, but never let it blind you to the winds of change.

CHAPTER III:

Conquering New Territories: Machiavelli's Mixed Principalities in the Modern Business Landscape

In "The Prince," Machiavelli's discusses mixed principalities - states that are newly acquired and added to existing domains. He argues that these are more challenging to maintain than hereditary states, as the ruler must navigate the complexities of integrating new territories with existing ones. This concept has striking parallels in today's business world, particularly in the realms of mergers and acquisitions, market expansion, and diversification strategies.

The Challenge of Integration

Machiavelli noted that when a prince acquires a new state that is similar in culture and customs to his existing one, it is easier to hold. However, if the new territory is significantly different, it becomes much more difficult to control and integrate.

In the modern business context, this translates directly to the challenges companies face when merging with or acquiring other businesses, or when expanding into new markets.

Consider the case of Daimler-Chrysler. In 1998, Daimler-Benz of Germany merged with Chrysler Corporation of the United States in what was touted as a "merger of equals." However, the cultural differences between the two companies proved insurmountable. The German engineering-driven culture clashed with the American sales-driven approach, leading to numerous conflicts and ultimately, the dissolution of the merger in 2007.

On the other hand, when Disney acquired Pixar in 2006, the integration was much smoother. Despite initial concerns, Disney recognized the unique culture that made Pixar successful and largely allowed it to operate independently. This approach aligns with Machiavelli's advice to respect the customs of newly acquired territories.

The Importance of Local Presence

Machiavelli advised that a prince should either reside in the new territory or establish colonies there. In today's globalized business world, this translates to the importance of establishing a strong local presence when entering new markets.

Amazon's expansion into India provides an interesting case study. Recognizing the unique challenges of the Indian market, Amazon didn't simply replicate its U.S. model. Instead, it adapted to local conditions, partnering with neighborhood stores for deliveries, offering cash on delivery options, and even creating a Hindi version of its app. This approach of "colonizing" the new market with a localized strategy has helped Amazon compete effectively against local rivals.

Similarly, when Walmart entered China, it adapted its store formats, product selections, and even its name (Walmart is known as "Wō'ērmǎ" in China) to suit local preferences. This strategy of adapting to local conditions while maintaining core strengths aligns with Machiavelli's advice for ruling mixed principalities.

Dealing with Opposition

Machiavelli observed that in newly acquired territories, there will always be some who resist the new ruler, either out of ambition or fear of change. He advised princes to identify and neutralize these potential threats quickly.

In the business world, this often plays out in the resistance to change during mergers and acquisitions. When Lenovo acquired IBM's personal computer business in 2005, it faced significant challenges in integrating IBM's corporate culture and retaining key employees. Lenovo addressed this by retaining many of IBM's top executives and maintaining separate headquarters in the U.S. and China, effectively neutralizing potential opposition and leveraging existing talent.

The Strategy of Division

Machiavelli suggested that a wise prince should create divisions in newly acquired territories to prevent unified opposition. While we can't endorse creating internal strife, we can interpret this in a more positive light for modern business: diversification.

Alphabet (Google's parent company) provides an excellent example of this strategy. By reorganizing into a conglomerate structure, Alphabet effectively "divided" its empire into more manageable units. This structure allows each division to operate with a degree of autonomy, reducing the risk of unified opposition to the parent company's strategies and allowing for more nimble responses to market changes in different sectors.

The Power of Anticipation

Machiavelli emphasized the importance of anticipating problems before they arise. He argued that addressing issues early is more effective than waiting for them to become severe.

In the business world, this principle is evident in the practice of scenario planning and risk management. Companies that successfully expand into new markets or integrate acquisitions often do so by thoroughly analyzing potential challenges beforehand.

For instance, when Vodafone entered India's telecom market, it anticipated regulatory challenges and fierce local competition. By partnering with a local company (Essar Group) initially and gradually increasing its stake, Vodafone managed a smoother entry into this complex market.

The Role of Timing

Machiavelli noted that the difficulties in acquiring a new territory are partly due to the change itself, as people are naturally resistant to new rulers. He advised that a prince should inflict all necessary hardships at once, rather than prolonging them over time.

In business terms, this translates to the importance of swift and decisive action when implementing major changes, such as post-merger integrations or significant strategic shifts.

When Microsoft acquired Nokia's mobile phone business in 2013, it initially maintained Nokia as a separate division. However, this prolonged the integration process and led to confusion in the market. In 2015, Microsoft made the decisive move to fully integrate Nokia, writing off the acquisition and laying off thousands of employees. While painful, this decisive action allowed Microsoft to refocus its mobile strategy more effectively.

Balancing Old and New

Machiavelli advised that in mixed principalities, a wise ruler should maintain some old institutions while establishing new ones. This balance helps to legitimize the new rule while also implementing necessary changes.

In the business world, this principle is often applied in post-merger integrations and corporate transformations. When Fiat acquired Chrysler in 2009, it didn't completely overhaul Chrysler's operations. Instead, it maintained key aspects of Chrysler's identity and operations while gradually implementing changes to improve efficiency and profitability.

Similarly, when IBM transformed from a hardware company to a services and cloud computing company, it didn't abandon its hardware business entirely. Instead, it gradually shifted focus while maintaining some of its traditional offerings, ensuring a smoother transition for both employees and customers.

The Importance of Local Allies

Machiavelli emphasized the importance of cultivating local supporters in newly acquired territories. He argued that these local allies could provide valuable insights and help maintain control.

In modern business, this translates to the importance of local partnerships and employees when entering new markets. When Starbucks entered China, it partnered with local companies to better understand the market and navigate regulatory challenges. It also adapted its offerings to local tastes, introducing products like green tea frappuccinos.

Uber's contrasting experiences in China and Southeast Asia illustrate this point. In China, Uber struggled to compete with local rival Didi Chuxing and eventually sold its Chinese operations. In Southeast Asia, Uber formed a strategic partnership with local player Grab, effectively maintaining a stake in the market while benefiting from Grab's local expertise.

Conclusion: The Enduring Relevance of Machiavelli's Mixed Principalities

Machiavelli's insights on mixed principalities offer valuable lessons for modern business leaders navigating mergers, acquisitions, and market expansions. The challenges of integrating new businesses or entering new markets are not dissimilar from those faced by Renaissance princes expanding their territories.

Key takeaways for modern leaders include:

1. Understand and respect local cultures and customs when entering new markets or acquiring companies.
2. Establish a strong local presence and adapt strategies to local conditions.
3. Anticipate and address potential opposition or challenges proactively.
4. Consider diversification as a strategy to manage a complex business "empire."
5. Act decisively when implementing major changes.
6. Balance maintaining existing structures with implementing new ones.
7. Cultivate local partnerships and talent for insights and support.

By applying these Machiavellian principles, modern business leaders can more effectively navigate the complex landscape of global business, successfully "conquering" and maintaining new territories in the corporate world. As with Machiavelli's princes, the key to success lies in strategic thinking, adaptability, and a nuanced understanding of the dynamics of power and culture.

CHAPTER IV:

The Self-Made Prince: Machiavelli's Lessons for Modern Entrepreneurs

Machiavelli discusses new principalities acquired through one's own arms and ability. He argues that while these are the most difficult to acquire, they are the most secure and honorable once established. This concept has a direct parallel in the modern business world, particularly in the realm of entrepreneurship and startup culture.

The Virtue of Self-Reliance

Machiavelli believed that rulers who came to power through their own skill and effort were more secure in their position. He cites examples like Moses, Cyrus, and Romulus - leaders who created new states through their own abilities.

In the modern business landscape, this principle is embodied in the ethos of the self-made entrepreneur. These are individuals who build companies from the ground up, relying on their own skills, vision, and determination.

Consider the case of Steve Jobs and Apple. Jobs, along with Steve Wozniak, built Apple from a garage startup to one of the world's most valuable companies. Jobs' vision, technical knowledge, and marketing acumen were crucial in establishing Apple's success. Even after being forced out of the company, his return and subsequent leadership cemented Apple's position as an industry leader.

Similarly, Elon Musk's journey with Tesla and SpaceX exemplifies the modern "prince" who acquires his "principality" through his own arms and ability. Musk's technical expertise, vision for sustainable energy and space exploration, and ability to attract talent and investment have been key to his companies' success.

The Challenge of Innovation

Machiavelli noted that those who rise to power through their own abilities face significant challenges. They must establish new systems and convince people to believe in something new, which is inherently difficult.

This mirrors the challenges faced by innovative startups and entrepreneurs. They often need to create entirely new markets or disrupt existing ones, which requires convincing consumers, investors, and sometimes regulators of the value of their new ideas.

Airbnb serves as a prime example. When Brian Chesky and his co-founders started the company, the idea of staying in strangers' homes seemed bizarre to many. They had to create trust mechanisms, navigate complex regulations, and change consumer behavior to establish their business model.

Similarly, when Netflix began offering streaming services, it faced skepticism about the viability of online video distribution. Reed Hastings and his team had to overcome technical challenges, negotiate with content providers, and essentially create a new market for streaming entertainment.

The Importance of Preparation

Machiavelli emphasized that successful leaders who rise through their own abilities are often preparing for their opportunity long before it arises. They cultivate the skills and resources needed to seize the moment when it comes.

In the startup world, this principle is evident in the concept of the "prepared mind." Successful entrepreneurs often have deep domain expertise or have been thinking about their business idea for years before launching.

Mark Zuckerberg, for instance, had been building social networking sites since his early college days before creating Facebook. His previous projects, like Facemash and CourseMatch, prepared him for the opportunity to create a global social network.

Similarly, Jeff Bezos worked on Wall Street and gained valuable insights into online commerce before starting Amazon. His preparation allowed him to seize the opportunity presented by the growing internet economy.

The Role of Execution

Machiavelli argued that while fortune might provide an opportunity, it's the leader's virtue (or ability) that determines whether that opportunity is successfully seized.

In business terms, this translates to the critical importance of execution. Many entrepreneurs have great ideas, but it's the ability to execute effectively that separates successful startups from failed ones.

Consider the case of Uber and its many competitors. While the idea of ride-hailing apps was not unique to Uber, the company's superior execution - including its aggressive expansion strategy, ability to attract drivers and riders, and continuous product improvements - allowed it to dominate the market in many countries.

The Challenges of Pioneering

Machiavelli noted that innovators make enemies of all those who prospered under the old system, while those who might benefit from the new system are initially lukewarm supporters at best.

This dynamic is clearly visible in disruptive startups. When Tesla began promoting electric vehicles, it faced strong opposition from traditional auto manufacturers and dealers. Similarly, cryptocurrency startups have faced resistance from established financial institutions and regulators.

However, Machiavelli also pointed out that once these innovators overcome initial resistance and prove their worth, they become more secure than hereditary princes. We see this in how companies like Amazon, Google, and Facebook, once disruptive startups, have become dominant forces in their industries.

The Importance of Self-Reliance

Machiavelli advised that princes who rise through their own abilities should rely on themselves rather than on others or on fortune. This principle is echoed in the startup world's emphasis on bootstrapping and maintaining control.

Many successful entrepreneurs have followed this path. For instance, Spanx founder Sara Blakely famously built her company without external investment, allowing her to maintain complete control and follow her vision. Similarly, Mailchimp's founders bootstrapped their company for 17 years before taking any outside investment, growing it into a multi-billion dollar business.

The Power of Vision

Machiavelli emphasized the importance of a clear vision for innovators. They need to be able to imagine a new order and convince others to believe in it.

This is particularly relevant in the tech startup world, where founders often need to paint a picture of a future that doesn't yet exist. Elon Musk's vision of sustainable energy and space colonization, or Mark Zuckerberg's vision of a connected world, have been crucial in attracting talent, investment, and customers to their ventures.

The Need for Adaptability

While Machiavelli stressed self-reliance, he also recognized the need for leaders to adapt to changing circumstances. This is particularly relevant in today's fast-paced business environment.

Successful entrepreneurs often need to pivot their business models in response to market feedback or changing conditions. Slack, for instance, began as an internal tool for a game development company before pivoting to become a widely-used communication platform for businesses.

The Responsibility of Leadership

Machiavelli noted that leaders who rise through their own abilities have a particular responsibility to establish good foundations for their new state. In the business world, this translates to creating strong company cultures and sustainable business practices.

Leaders like Yvon Chouinard of Patagonia or Blake Mycoskie of TOMS have taken this to heart, building companies that prioritize social and environmental responsibility alongside profitability.

Conclusion: The Modern Self-Made Prince

Machiavelli's insights on leaders who acquire power through their own arms and ability are remarkably applicable to modern entrepreneurs. The challenges of innovation, the importance of preparation and execution, the need for a clear vision, and the value of self-reliance are as relevant today as they were in Renaissance Italy.

Key takeaways for modern entrepreneurs include:

1. Cultivate deep domain expertise and prepare thoroughly before launching a venture.
2. Recognize that introducing innovations will face resistance, and prepare strategies to overcome it.
3. Focus on excellent execution, not just good ideas.
4. Maintain self-reliance and control where possible, but be willing to adapt when necessary.
5. Develop a clear, compelling vision that can inspire

others.
6. Recognize the responsibilities that come with success, including establishing strong foundations for long-term sustainability.

By applying these Machiavellian principles, modern entrepreneurs can navigate the challenging path of building new ventures. Like Machiavelli's self-made princes, today's successful founders combine vision, skill, and determination to create new realities in the business world.

CHAPTER V:

Fortune's Favorites: Machiavelli's Lessons on Inherited Success in Modern Business

Machiavelli discusses those who become rulers through good fortune or the power of others. He argues that while these principalities are easy to acquire, they are difficult to maintain. This concept has intriguing parallels in today's business world, particularly in the realms of inherited businesses, sudden market opportunities, and externally-funded startups.

The Gift of Fortune

Machiavelli observed that those who come to power through good fortune or the favor of others often struggle to maintain their position. They haven't developed the skills and experience necessary to rule effectively.

In the business world, this can be likened to inherited companies, unexpected market windfalls, or startups that achieve rapid success through external funding rather than organic growth.

Consider the case of Theranos and its founder, Elizabeth Holmes. Holmes, backed by powerful investors and board members, rapidly built Theranos into a company valued at $9 billion. However, the lack of a viable product and Holmes' inexperience in the medical field eventually led to the company's downfall. This mirrors Machiavelli's warning about the precariousness of power gained through fortune rather than ability.

The Challenges of Inherited Success

Machiavelli noted that those who inherit power often lack the skills to maintain it. This principle is often evident in family businesses passed down through generations.

The cautionary tale of the Gucci family illustrates this point. By the 1980s, the third generation of the Gucci family was running the company. Internal conflicts, mismanagement, and a lack of strategic vision led to a near-bankruptcy situation. It took an external CEO, Domenico De Sole, and designer Tom Ford to revitalize the brand in the 1990s.

On the other hand, the Mars family provides a more positive example. The Mars company has successfully transitioned through multiple generations by prioritizing family member education and bringing in professional management when needed. This approach aligns with Machiavelli's advice that fortunate princes must quickly learn the skills necessary to maintain their position.

The Double-Edged Sword of External Support

Machiavelli warned that rulers who come to power through the support of others are dependent on their continued goodwill. In the startup world, this dynamic is often seen in the relationship between founders and venture capitalists.

WeWork's rise and fall under Adam Neumann exemplifies this principle. Backed by massive investments from SoftBank, WeWork achieved a peak valuation of $47 billion. However, when investors lost confidence in Neumann's leadership, the company's valuation plummeted, and Neumann was ousted as CEO.

Conversely, companies like Zoom have managed to use external funding wisely while maintaining a strong, founder-led culture. Zoom's CEO, Eric Yuan, balanced investor interests with a clear vision and solid business fundamentals, leading to sustainable growth.

The Importance of Laying Foundations

Machiavelli advised that those who come to power through fortune must quickly lay strong foundations for their rule. In business terms, this translates to establishing solid business practices, corporate culture, and strategic vision.

Facebook (now Meta) provides an interesting case study. While Mark Zuckerberg's initial success with Facebook could be partly attributed to fortunate timing and circumstances, he quickly established strong foundations. He brought in experienced executives like Sheryl Sandberg, developed a clear long-term vision, and built a culture of "move fast and break things" that helped the company maintain its competitive edge.

The Need for Adaptability

Machiavelli noted that fortunate princes must be able to

adapt quickly to changing circumstances. In the business world, this principle is crucial for companies that find sudden success.

Pokémon Go, developed by Niantic, is a prime example. The game became an overnight global phenomenon in 2016. However, Niantic had to rapidly scale its infrastructure, address security concerns, and continue innovating to maintain its user base. The company's ability to adapt quickly to its unexpected success was crucial in capitalizing on its initial good fortune.

The Value of Mentorship

While not explicitly mentioned by Machiavelli, the modern equivalent of his advice for fortunate princes to quickly learn the arts of rule could be seen in the importance of mentorship in business.

When Google's founders, Larry Page and Sergey Brin, found themselves at the helm of a rapidly growing company, they brought in Eric Schmidt as CEO. Schmidt's experience helped guide the young company through its high-growth phase and IPO. This decision aligns with Machiavelli's advice for fortunate rulers to quickly acquire the necessary skills to maintain their position.

The Risks of Complacency

Machiavelli warned that those who come to power easily often fail to appreciate the precariousness of their position. In the business world, this can manifest as complacency in the face of changing market conditions.

Blockbuster's failure to adapt to the rise of streaming services is a classic example. The company's dominant position in the video rental market led to complacency, allowing Netflix to disrupt the industry. This aligns with Machiavelli's warning that fortune is fickle and those who rely on it must be constantly vigilant.

The Power of Timing

While Machiavelli was skeptical of fortune, he recognized that timing plays a crucial role in success. In the business world, being in the right place at the right time can lead to extraordinary opportunities.

Airbnb's success was partly due to fortunate timing. The company launched just as the 2008 financial crisis was making people more open to alternative, cost-effective travel accommodations. However, the founders' ability to capitalize on this timing through effective execution was crucial to the company's long-term success.

The Importance of Self-Reliance

Machiavelli advised that fortunate princes should quickly learn to rely on themselves rather than others. In the business world, this principle is often seen in founders who maintain control of their companies even as they grow.

Jeff Bezos' leadership of Amazon exemplifies this principle. While Amazon benefited from fortunate timing during the dot-com boom, Bezos maintained a controlling stake in the company and continued to shape its strategy directly. This allowed Amazon to pursue long-term goals, often at the expense of short-term profits, leading to its current dominant position.

Conclusion: Navigating the Winds of Fortune in Modern Business

Machiavelli's insights on leaders who acquire power through fortune offer valuable lessons for modern business leaders who find themselves in positions of sudden or inherited success. The challenges of maintaining power gained easily, the importance of quickly establishing strong foundations, and the need for adaptability and self-reliance are as relevant today as they were in Renaissance Italy.

Key takeaways for modern business leaders include:

1. Recognize that sudden or inherited success comes with unique challenges.
2. Quickly establish strong business foundations and corporate culture.
3. Be adaptable and ready to pivot in response to changing circumstances.
4. Seek mentorship and rapidly develop necessary leadership skills.
5. Avoid complacency and constantly innovate.
6. Capitalize on fortunate timing but don't rely solely on it.
7. Strive for self-reliance and maintain control over key strategic decisions.

By applying these Machiavellian principles, modern business leaders can better navigate the challenges that come with sudden success or inherited positions. Like Machiavelli's fortunate princes, today's leaders must recognize that while fortune may open doors, it's their own actions and decisions that ultimately determine long-term success.

CHAPTER VI:

The Dark Side of Success: Machiavelli's Lessons on Unethical Practices in Modern Business

Machiavelli discusses those who come to power through wicked or unethical means. While he doesn't endorse such methods, he analyzes them dispassionately, noting that they can be effective if applied swiftly and not repeated. This concept has controversial but undeniable parallels in the modern business world, particularly in the realms of aggressive business tactics, ethical breaches, and corporate malfeasance.

The Effectiveness of Ruthlessness

Machiavelli observed that swift, decisive actions, even if considered cruel, can be effective in establishing and maintaining power. He cites the example of Agathocles of Sicily, who rose to power through violence and treachery but managed to rule successfully for many years.

In the business world, this principle can be seen in

aggressive corporate tactics that, while not illegal, may be considered unethical or ruthless.

Consider the case of Uber under its co-founder and former CEO, Travis Kalanick. Uber's rapid rise to dominance in the ride-hailing industry was marked by a series of controversial tactics:

1. The "Greyball" program to evade law enforcement in cities where Uber was not yet approved.
2. Aggressive poaching of drivers from competitors.
3. A culture that often ignored sexual harassment complaints.

These tactics, while ethically questionable, contributed to Uber's rapid growth and market dominance. However, as Machiavelli might have predicted, the accumulation of scandals eventually led to Kalanick's ouster and a major company overhaul.

The Dangers of Repeated Cruelty

Machiavelli warned that while initial cruelties might be overlooked if followed by good governance, continued unethical behavior would lead to a ruler's downfall. This principle is evident in companies that engage in ongoing unethical practices.

Enron's collapse provides a stark example. The energy company's leadership engaged in systematic accounting fraud, inflating profits and hiding debts. While these practices initially led to soaring stock prices, the continued deception eventually resulted in one of the largest corporate bankruptcies in U.S. history and criminal convictions for its top executives.

The Importance of Swift Action

Machiavelli argued that if unethical actions are necessary, they should be done swiftly and all at once, rather than prolonged over time. In the business world, this could be interpreted as the importance of decisive action in crisis situations.

Johnson & Johnson's handling of the Tylenol crisis in 1982 provides a positive example of swift, decisive action. When seven people died after taking cyanide-laced Tylenol, J&J immediately recalled all Tylenol products nationwide, despite the enormous cost. This decisive action, while painful in the short term, helped restore public trust in the company and the brand.

The Long-Term Consequences of Unethical Behavior

Machiavelli noted that while unethical actions might bring short-term gains, they often lead to long-term instability. This is particularly relevant in today's business world, where information travels fast and corporate reputations can be quickly tarnished.

The Volkswagen emissions scandal illustrates this principle. VW's decision to install software to cheat emissions tests initially allowed them to sell more "clean diesel" cars. However, when the deception was uncovered in 2015, it led to billions in fines, a massive recall, and severe damage to the company's reputation that persists years later.

The Role of Corporate Culture

While Machiavelli focused on individual rulers, in modern business, unethical practices often stem from problematic corporate cultures. Wells Fargo's fake accounts scandal, where employees opened millions of unauthorized accounts to meet aggressive sales targets, exemplifies how a culture that prioritizes results over ethics can lead to widespread malfeasance.

The Importance of Ethical Leadership

Machiavelli argued that a leader's actions set the tone for the entire state. In the corporate world, this translates to the crucial role of ethical leadership in shaping company culture and practices.

Microsoft's transformation under Satya Nadella provides a positive example. Nadella shifted the company's culture from the aggressive, competition-focused approach of his predecessors to one emphasizing empathy and collaboration. This ethical shift has corresponded with a period of renewed growth and innovation for the company.

The Power of Redemption

While Machiavelli didn't discuss redemption explicitly, the modern business world provides examples of companies that have rebounded from ethical lapses through concerted efforts to reform.

General Electric's transformation under Jack Welch in the 1980s and 1990s involved aggressive tactics like mass layoffs and creative accounting practices. However, subsequent leaders have worked to reshape GE's culture and practices, emphasizing ethical behavior and sustainability.

The Role of Regulation and Oversight

Machiavelli wrote in a time of relatively weak central

authority. In contrast, modern businesses operate in an environment of complex regulations and oversight. Companies that engage in unethical practices now face potential legal consequences as well as public backlash.

The breakup of Standard Oil in 1911 due to monopolistic practices, and more recent antitrust actions against tech giants like Google and Facebook, demonstrate the role of regulatory oversight in curbing unethical business practices.

The Ethical Minefield of Disruption

In the modern business world, particularly in tech, the mantra of "move fast and break things" can sometimes lead companies into ethical gray areas. While not explicitly "wicked," disruptive innovation can challenge existing regulations and societal norms.

Airbnb's impact on housing markets and Uber's classification of drivers as contractors rather than employees are examples of how disruptive business models can raise ethical questions, even if the companies' intentions are not explicitly malicious.

The Importance of Stakeholder Consideration

While Machiavelli focused primarily on maintaining power, modern business ethics emphasize the importance of considering all stakeholders, not just shareholders. Companies that neglect this principle often face backlash.

Amazon, despite its business success, has faced criticism for its treatment of warehouse workers and its environmental impact. This has led to increased pressure for the company to address these ethical concerns, showing how neglecting stakeholder interests can create long-term challenges.

Conclusion: Navigating the Ethical Landscape of Modern Business

Machiavelli's analysis of power acquired through wickedness offers sobering lessons for modern business leaders. While few would openly advocate for unethical practices, the pressures of competition and the drive for growth can sometimes lead companies down ethically questionable paths.

Key takeaways for modern business leaders include:

1. Recognize that unethical practices, even if initially successful, often lead to long-term negative consequences.
2. If decisive action is necessary in a crisis, act swiftly and transparently.
3. Understand that corporate culture plays a crucial role in ethical behavior.
4. Emphasize ethical leadership to set the tone for the entire organization.
5. Be aware of the regulatory environment and the consequences of non-compliance.
6. Consider all stakeholders, not just shareholders, in decision-making.
7. If ethical lapses occur, take genuine steps towards reform and redemption.

By applying these principles, modern business leaders can navigate the complex ethical landscape of today's business world. Like Machiavelli's princes, they must balance the drive for success with the need for ethical governance, recognizing that true, lasting success is built on a foundation of integrity and trust.

It's crucial to note that while we can learn from Machiavelli's analysis, his amoral approach to power should not be taken as an endorsement of unethical behavior. In today's interconnected world, ethical business practices are not just morally right, but often essential for long-term success and sustainability.

CHAPTER VII:

The People's Choice: Civic Principalities in Modern Corporate Governance

Machiavelli discusses civic principalities - states where the ruler comes to power through the support of his fellow citizens. He argues that such a ruler must carefully balance the interests of the people and the nobles (or elite). This concept has intriguing parallels in modern business, particularly in areas of corporate governance, stakeholder management, and leadership in democratic or cooperative business structures.

The Power of Popular Support

Machiavelli observed that a ruler who comes to power with the support of the common people has a more stable foundation than one who relies solely on the nobility. In the business world, this principle can be seen in the importance of employee engagement and customer loyalty.

Consider the case of Costco. The company's CEO, Craig Jelinek, has maintained a policy of paying workers well above industry averages and providing comprehensive benefits. This approach has resulted in high employee satisfaction, low turnover, and strong customer loyalty. Costco's success demonstrates how "popular" support from employees and customers can create a stable foundation for a business.

Balancing Stakeholder Interests

Machiavelli noted that a civic prince must balance the interests of the people and the nobles. In modern business terms, this translates to managing the interests of various stakeholders - employees, customers, shareholders, and the broader community.

Unilever under Paul Polman's leadership provides an excellent example. Polman implemented the Unilever Sustainable Living Plan, which aimed to double the company's size while reducing its environmental impact and increasing its positive social impact. This approach sought to balance the interests of shareholders (growth) with those of employees, consumers, and society at large (sustainability and social responsibility).

The Challenges of Democratic Leadership

Machiavelli discussed the challenges of ruling in a state where the people have a strong voice. This has parallels in modern cooperative businesses and companies with strong employee ownership.

The John Lewis Partnership in the UK, which operates department stores and supermarkets, is owned by its employees (called Partners). The company's constitution establishes a partnership council and gives employees a say in major decisions. While this democratic structure can lead to more engaged employees, it also presents challenges in swift decision-making and maintaining a unified direction.

The Importance of Adaptability

Machiavelli advised that a ruler in a civic principality must be adaptable, able to shift between severity and indulgence as circumstances require. In the business world, this principle is evident in leaders who can adjust their management style to changing market conditions and organizational needs.

Microsoft's transformation under Satya Nadella exemplifies this adaptability. Nadella shifted the company's culture from the top-down, competitive approach of his predecessors to a more collaborative, innovative culture. This adaptability has corresponded with a period of renewed growth and innovation for Microsoft.

The Power of Transparency

While Machiavelli is often associated with secrecy and manipulation, he recognized the value of transparency in civic principalities. In modern business, transparency has become increasingly important, particularly in building trust with employees and customers.

Patagonia, the outdoor clothing company, provides an excellent example of corporate transparency. The company's "Footprint Chronicles" initiative provides detailed information about its supply chain and environmental impact. This transparency has helped build strong customer loyalty and employee engagement.

The Role of Vision and Purpose

Machiavelli emphasized the importance of a ruler having a clear vision for the state. In modern business, this translates to the power of a strong corporate purpose or mission.

Unilever again provides a good example. Its purpose, "to make sustainable living commonplace," has guided the company's strategy and helped align the interests of various stakeholders. This clear purpose has contributed to Unilever's strong performance and reputation.

The Importance of Meritocracy

Machiavelli advised that a civic prince should reward merit to maintain the support of the people. In the business world, this principle is evident in companies that emphasize meritocracy and provide clear paths for advancement.

Google's early career development practices, including its famous "20% time" policy (where engineers could spend 20% of their time on personal projects), exemplify this approach. By rewarding innovation and providing opportunities for growth, Google has been able to attract and retain top talent.

The Challenge of Succession

Machiavelli noted that civic principalities face challenges in succession, as the people are accustomed to freedom. In the business world, this is evident in the difficulties many companies face in leadership transitions, particularly in founder-led companies.

Apple's transition after Steve Jobs provides an interesting case study. Tim Cook faced the challenge of maintaining Apple's innovative culture and market leadership while transitioning to a different leadership style. The company's continued success demonstrates how effective succession planning can overcome these challenges.

The Power of Institutional Structures

Machiavelli advised creating institutional structures to maintain stability in civic principalities. In the corporate world, this principle is evident in the importance of strong corporate governance structures.

The scandal at Theranos, where weak board oversight allowed fraudulent practices to continue unchecked, demonstrates the dangers of inadequate governance structures. In contrast, companies like Berkshire Hathaway, with its strong and independent board, show how robust governance can contribute to long-term stability and success.

The Importance of Community Engagement

Machiavelli recognized that rulers of civic principalities needed to maintain strong connections with their communities. In modern business, this principle is evident in corporate social responsibility (CSR) initiatives and community engagement programs.

Salesforce's 1-1-1 model, where the company commits 1% of equity, 1% of product, and 1% of employee time to philanthropic causes, exemplifies this approach. This model has helped Salesforce build strong relationships with the communities where it operates, contributing to its positive reputation and employee satisfaction.

Conclusion: The Modern Civic Corporation

Machiavelli's insights on civic principalities offer valuable lessons for modern business leaders, particularly those leading companies with strong stakeholder engagement or democratic structures. The challenges of balancing diverse interests, maintaining popular support, and creating stable yet adaptable organizations are as relevant today as they were in Renaissance Italy.

Key takeaways for modern business leaders include:

1. Recognize the power of broad stakeholder support, including employees and customers.
2. Balance the interests of various stakeholders, including shareholders, employees, customers, and the broader community.
3. Be adaptable in leadership style and business strategy.
4. Embrace transparency to build trust and engagement.
5. Develop and communicate a clear corporate purpose or vision.
6. Implement meritocratic practices to attract and retain talent.
7. Plan carefully for leadership succession.
8. Establish strong corporate governance structures.
9. Engage actively with the broader community through CSR initiatives.

By applying these principles, modern business leaders can create more resilient, engaged, and successful organizations. Like Machiavelli's civic prince, they must navigate the complex landscape of diverse stakeholder interests, building organizations that can thrive with the support of their "citizens" - employees, customers, and communities.

CHAPTER VIII:

The Untouchables: Machiavelli's Ecclesiastical Principalities in Modern Business

Machiavelli discusses ecclesiastical principalities, referring to the papal states of his time. He observes that these states are unique in that they are sustained by long-standing institutions and religious doctrines, making them exceptionally stable regardless of the ruler's conduct. This concept has interesting parallels in the modern business world, particularly in industries with high barriers to entry, companies with strong brand loyalty, or organizations with unique cultural or ideological foundations.

The Power of Established Institutions

Machiavelli noted that ecclesiastical principalities are maintained by ancient religious institutions, which are so powerful that they keep their rulers in power regardless of how they behave. In the business world, this can be likened to companies with exceptionally strong brand recognition or market dominance.

Consider the case of Coca-Cola. Despite occasional controversies and changing consumer preferences towards healthier options, Coca-Cola's brand power and global distribution network have allowed it to maintain market leadership for over a century. The strength of its brand and infrastructure acts much like the religious institutions Machiavelli described, providing stability regardless of short-term leadership decisions.

The Influence of Ideology

Ecclesiastical principalities were underpinned by religious doctrine, which provided a powerful ideological foundation. In the business world, this can be seen in companies with strong corporate cultures or ideological missions.

Apple under Steve Jobs is a prime example. Jobs cultivated a quasi-religious devotion to Apple's products and design philosophy. This ideological foundation has allowed Apple to maintain a loyal customer base and premium pricing even in highly competitive markets. The company's emphasis on design, user experience, and ecosystem integration acts as a kind of "doctrine" that sustains its market position.

The Challenge of Disruption

Machiavelli observed that ecclesiastical principalities were exceptionally difficult to challenge or overthrow. In the business world, this principle is evident in industries with high barriers to entry or companies with near-monopoly status.

Microsoft's dominance in personal computer operating systems illustrates this concept. Despite numerous challenges over the years, Windows has maintained its market leadership due to its entrenched position and the difficulty of displacing such a widely-used system. However, the rise of mobile operating systems like iOS and Android shows that even such entrenched positions can eventually face disruption.

The Role of Tradition

Ecclesiastical principalities relied heavily on tradition and custom. In the business world, this can be seen in companies that leverage their heritage as a key part of their brand identity.

Luxury brands like Louis Vuitton or Hermès exemplify this principle. These companies rely heavily on their long histories and traditions of craftsmanship to justify premium pricing and maintain customer loyalty. Their heritage acts as a form of "doctrine" that supports their market position.

The Power of Network Effects

While not explicitly mentioned by Machiavelli, the stability of ecclesiastical principalities has parallels with modern businesses that benefit from strong network effects.

Facebook (now Meta) provides a good example. The more users that join the platform, the more valuable it becomes for all users, creating a self-reinforcing cycle that makes it difficult for competitors to challenge Facebook's dominance in social networking. This network effect acts much like the self-sustaining nature of ecclesiastical power that Machiavelli described.

The Importance of Regulatory Environments

Ecclesiastical principalities benefited from a unique regulatory status. In the modern business world, some companies or industries enjoy similar protections or advantages due to regulatory environments.

The pharmaceutical industry, with its patent protections and high regulatory barriers to entry, illustrates this principle. Companies like Pfizer or Johnson & Johnson benefit from a regulatory environment that provides periods of market exclusivity for new drugs, allowing them to recoup research and development costs.

The Challenge of Ethical Leadership

Machiavelli noted that rulers of ecclesiastical principalities could maintain power regardless of their conduct. While this isn't entirely true in modern business, some companies have shown remarkable resilience in the face of ethical scandals.

Wells Fargo's fake accounts scandal provides an example. Despite creating millions of fraudulent accounts, the bank's entrenched position in the U.S. financial system allowed it to weather the storm and maintain a significant market presence. However, the long-term reputational damage and regulatory consequences show that modern businesses aren't entirely immune to the consequences of unethical behavior.

The Role of Intangible Assets

The power of ecclesiastical principalities often lay in

intangible factors like faith and tradition. In modern business, intangible assets like brand value, patents, and intellectual property play a similar role.

Google's search algorithm is a prime example. The company's dominance in search is largely due to its superior technology and data - intangible assets that are difficult for competitors to replicate. This creates a form of "ecclesiastical" power in the search market.

The Importance of Customer Loyalty

Religious devotion in ecclesiastical principalities has parallels with extreme customer loyalty in some modern businesses.

Tesla's customers often display a level of brand loyalty that goes beyond typical consumer behavior, defending the company and its CEO Elon Musk even in the face of controversies or product issues. This "faith" in the brand provides Tesla with a degree of insulation from normal market pressures.

The Power of Ecosystems

Ecclesiastical principalities were part of a broader religious ecosystem. In modern business, some companies have created powerful ecosystems that enhance their stability and market power.

Apple's ecosystem of devices, software, and services is a prime example. The interconnectedness of Apple's products creates a form of lock-in that makes it difficult for customers to switch to competitors, providing Apple with a form of "ecclesiastical" stability in the tech market.

Conclusion: The Modern "Ecclesiastical" Corporation

Machiavelli's insights on ecclesiastical principalities offer valuable lessons for modern business leaders, particularly those in industries with high barriers to entry or companies with strong brand identities. The power of established institutions, ideology, tradition, and intangible assets in creating stable and resilient businesses is as relevant today as it was in Renaissance Italy.

Key takeaways for modern business leaders include:

1. Recognize the power of strong brand identity and corporate culture in creating business resilience.
2. Understand the value of tradition and heritage in certain industries.
3. Be aware of the power of network effects and ecosystems in creating defensible market positions.
4. Leverage intangible assets like intellectual property and brand value.
5. Foster strong customer loyalty, but don't take it for granted.
6. Understand the role of regulatory environments in shaping competitive landscapes.
7. Recognize that even seemingly unassailable market positions can face disruption.
8. Remember that ethical behavior remains crucial, despite any market advantages.

By applying these principles, modern business leaders can create more resilient and enduring organizations. Like Machiavelli's ecclesiastical princes, they can leverage powerful institutional forces to maintain their market positions. However, they must also remain vigilant against complacency and potential disruption, recognizing that in the modern business world, no position of power is truly eternal.

CHAPTER IX:

Building Your Own Army: Machiavelli's Military Wisdom in Modern Business

Machiavelli discusses military organizations and the use of mercenaries. He strongly advises against relying on mercenary or auxiliary troops, arguing that a prince should build and rely on his own army. This concept has interesting parallels in the modern business world, particularly in areas of human resources, outsourcing, and core competencies.

The Dangers of Mercenaries

Machiavelli warned that mercenaries are unreliable, lacking loyalty and fighting spirit. In the business world, this can be likened to over-reliance on external consultants or temporary workers for core functions.

Consider the case of IBM in the 1990s. Under CEO Louis Gerstner, IBM realized it had become too dependent on external consultants for its core IT services business. This led to a strategic shift towards building internal capabilities and reducing reliance on outsourced talent. By developing its own "army" of skilled consultants, IBM was able to better control quality and build deeper client relationships.

The Importance of Core Competencies

Machiavelli argued that a prince should personally lead his troops and understand the art of war. In business terms, this translates to leaders having a deep understanding of their company's core competencies and being actively involved in key operations.

Apple under Steve Jobs exemplifies this principle. Jobs was deeply involved in product development and design, which he saw as Apple's core competency. His hands-on approach and insistence on keeping key functions in-house contributed significantly to Apple's innovative products and success.

The Risks of Outsourcing

Machiavelli cautioned against relying on auxiliary troops (borrowed from allies), as they could become a threat if they grew too strong. This has parallels in the business risks associated with outsourcing critical functions.

Boeing's experience with the 787 Dreamliner illustrates this point. The company outsourced an unprecedented amount of the aircraft's design and manufacturing to external suppliers. This led to significant delays, quality issues, and loss of control over the project. Boeing learned the hard way the importance of maintaining core competencies in-house.

Building a Loyal Workforce

Machiavelli emphasized the importance of having one's own army, loyal to the state. In the business world, this translates to building a committed and engaged workforce.

Southwest Airlines is renowned for its strong company culture and employee loyalty. The company's approach to hiring for attitude and training for skill, along with its profit-sharing program, has created a workforce that consistently delivers high customer satisfaction. This "loyal army" has been a key factor in Southwest's long-term success in the highly competitive airline industry.

The Value of Training and Development

Machiavelli advised princes to keep their armies exercised in times of peace. In business, this principle is evident in companies that invest heavily in employee training and development.

Google's approach to employee development is a good example. The company offers numerous learning opportunities, from formal classes to peer-to-peer learning programs. This continuous "exercise" keeps Google's workforce sharp and innovative, contributing to the company's technological leadership.

The Importance of Leadership

Machiavelli stressed that a prince should lead his army personally. In the corporate world, this principle is reflected in leaders who are deeply involved in their company's operations and lead by example.

Elon Musk's hands-on leadership at Tesla and SpaceX exemplifies this approach. Musk is known for his deep involvement in engineering and design decisions, often working alongside his employees. This direct leadership has been crucial in driving innovation and overcoming challenges in both companies.

The Dangers of Overreliance on Technology

While Machiavelli didn't discuss technology, his warnings about overreliance on external forces can be applied to modern businesses' dependence on technology.

The 2010 "flash crash" in the U.S. stock market, partly caused by algorithmic trading, illustrates the dangers of overreliance on automated systems. Just as Machiavelli warned against trusting mercenaries, modern businesses must be cautious about blindly trusting technology without human oversight.

The Importance of Adaptability

Machiavelli advised princes to adapt their military strategies to the nature of the terrain. In business, this translates to the importance of adapting strategies to different market conditions.

Netflix's evolution from a DVD-by-mail service to a streaming platform to a content creator demonstrates this adaptability. By "changing terrain" as technology and consumer preferences shifted, Netflix has maintained its market leadership.

The Value of Self-Reliance

Machiavelli's overall message was one of self-reliance - a prince should not depend on external forces for the security of his state. In business, this principle is reflected in companies that maintain control over their key value-creating activities.

Vertically integrated companies like Apple (which controls everything from chip design to retail stores) or Tesla (which produces many components in-house) exemplify this self-reliance. By controlling critical aspects of their value chain, these companies can ensure quality, drive innovation, and respond quickly to market changes.

The Role of Corporate Culture

While not explicitly discussed by Machiavelli, a strong corporate culture can act as a unifying force similar to the loyalty Machiavelli sought in his ideal army.

Zappos, the online shoe retailer, is known for its strong corporate culture centered on customer service. This culture acts as a binding force, creating a loyal and committed workforce that delivers exceptional customer experiences.

The Importance of Agility

Machiavelli stressed the importance of having a flexible and mobile army. In the business world, this translates to organizational agility - the ability to respond quickly to market changes.

Amazon's ability to rapidly enter and disrupt new markets - from books to cloud computing to groceries - demonstrates this agility. Like a well-trained army, Amazon can quickly mobilize resources to seize new opportunities.

Conclusion: Building Your Corporate Army

Machiavelli's insights on military organizations offer valuable lessons for modern business leaders. The importance of building internal capabilities, maintaining core competencies, fostering employee loyalty, and being adaptable to changing conditions are as relevant in today's corporate battlefields as they were in Renaissance Italy's literal ones.

Key takeaways for modern business leaders include:

1. Be cautious about over-relying on external consultants or outsourcing core functions.
2. Invest in building and maintaining core competencies.
3. Foster a loyal and engaged workforce through strong corporate culture and employee development.
4. Leaders should be deeply involved in and knowledgeable about key operations.
5. Continuously train and develop your workforce to stay competitive.
6. Be adaptable to changing market conditions.
7. Maintain self-reliance in key value-creating activities.
8. Cultivate organizational agility to respond quickly to opportunities and threats.

By applying these principles, modern business leaders can create more resilient, innovative, and successful organizations. Like Machiavelli's ideal prince, they can build and lead their own "armies," capable of defending their market position and conquering new territories in the ever-changing landscape of modern business.

CHAPTER X:

The Art of Leadership: Machiavelli's Princely Qualities in Modern Business

Machiavelli discusses the qualities a ruler should possess or appear to possess. He argues that while it's ideal to have positive qualities, a ruler must be prepared to act against these virtues when necessary for the state's benefit. This concept has profound implications for modern business leadership, touching on issues of ethics, public perception, and strategic decision-making.

The Balance of Virtue and Pragmatism

Machiavelli famously stated that it's better for a leader to be feared than loved if he cannot be both. In the business world, this translates to the balance between being respected and being liked.

Consider the leadership style of Jack Welch during his tenure as CEO of General Electric. Welch was known for his tough, results-oriented approach, which earned him the nickname "Neutron Jack" due to his willingness to eliminate underperforming employees and divisions. While not always loved, Welch was respected for his ability to drive results, and under his leadership, GE's value increased by 4,000%.

The Importance of Perception

Machiavelli advised that a prince should appear merciful, faithful, and religious, even if he cannot always act that way. In modern business, this relates to the importance of corporate image and reputation management.

Mark Zuckerberg's response to the Cambridge Analytica scandal provides an interesting case study. Despite Facebook's initial slow response, Zuckerberg eventually adopted a public persona of contrition and commitment to user privacy. Whether this image accurately reflected Facebook's internal practices is debatable, but it demonstrates the importance of managing public perception in times of crisis.

The Virtue of Adaptability

Machiavelli emphasized the importance of adapting one's behavior to the times. In the business world, this translates to the need for leaders to be flexible and responsive to changing market conditions.

Satya Nadella's leadership at Microsoft exemplifies this principle. Nadella shifted Microsoft's culture and strategy to embrace cloud computing and open-source software, moving away from the Windows-centric approach of his predecessors. This adaptability has led to a resurgence in Microsoft's growth and stock price.

The Balance of Generosity and Parsimony

Machiavelli discussed the virtues and dangers of generosity, warning that excessive generosity can lead to higher taxes and resentment. In business terms, this relates to managing company resources and stakeholder expectations.

Jeff Bezos' approach at Amazon demonstrates this balance. While Amazon is known for its customer-centric approach (a form of generosity), it's also famous for its frugal corporate culture. This balance has allowed Amazon to invest heavily in growth while maintaining profitability.

The Use of Cruelty

Machiavelli argued that cruelty, if used well, could be more merciful in the long run than misplaced compassion. While we shouldn't endorse cruelty in modern business, this principle can be seen in leaders making tough decisions for long-term benefit.

Steve Jobs' return to Apple in 1997 provides an example. Jobs made the difficult decision to drastically cut Apple's product line and lay off thousands of employees. While painful in the short term, these decisions were crucial in turning Apple around and setting the stage for its future success.

The Importance of Avoiding Hatred

Machiavelli warned that while a prince might not be loved, he must avoid being hated at all costs. In the business world, this translates to the importance of maintaining stakeholder goodwill.

Howard Schultz's leadership at Starbucks demonstrates this principle. Despite being a large corporation, Starbucks has maintained a positive image through initiatives like providing health insurance to part-time workers and ethical sourcing of coffee beans. These actions help Starbucks avoid the kind of public backlash that many large corporations face.

The Value of Keeping Promises

Machiavelli noted that while a prince shouldn't always keep his word, he should appear to do so. In modern business, this relates to the importance of managing expectations and maintaining credibility.

Warren Buffett's leadership at Berkshire Hathaway exemplifies the value of keeping promises and maintaining credibility. Buffett is known for his straightforward communication with shareholders and his long-term approach to investing. This consistency has earned him a reputation for trustworthiness, which has been a key factor in Berkshire Hathaway's success.

The Importance of Understanding Human Nature

Machiavelli emphasized the importance of understanding human nature to lead effectively. In the business world, this translates to emotional intelligence and the ability to motivate and manage people.

Mary Barra's leadership at General Motors demonstrates this principle. Barra has been praised for her ability to connect with employees at all levels and drive cultural change within GM. Her understanding of human nature has been crucial in navigating GM through challenges like the ignition switch recall crisis.

The Balance of Boldness and Caution

Machiavelli advised princes to be both bold and cautious, knowing when to act decisively and when to be patient. In business, this relates to strategic decision-making and risk management.

Elon Musk's leadership at Tesla and SpaceX demonstrates this balance. Musk is known for bold, visionary goals, but he also employs careful engineering processes and iterative development. This combination of boldness and caution has allowed his companies to achieve breakthroughs in electric vehicles and space technology.

The Importance of Surrounding Oneself with Good Advisors

Machiavelli stressed the importance of choosing wise counselors and avoiding flatterers. In modern business, this translates to building strong executive teams and fostering a culture of open communication.

Alan Mulally's turnaround of Ford Motor Company illustrates this principle. Mulally fostered a culture of transparency and teamwork among his executive team, encouraging open discussion of problems. This approach was crucial in navigating Ford through the 2008 financial crisis without government bailouts.

Conclusion: The Modern Machiavellian Leader

Machiavelli's insights on leadership qualities offer valuable lessons for modern business leaders. While some of his more ruthless advice may not be directly applicable, the underlying principles of balancing competing demands, managing perception, and making tough decisions for long-term benefit remain highly relevant.

Key takeaways for modern business leaders include:

1. Balance being respected with being liked; prioritize respect if you can't have both.
2. Manage public perception, especially during crises.
3. Be adaptable to changing market conditions.
4. Balance generosity with financial prudence.
5. Be prepared to make tough decisions for long-term benefit.
6. Maintain stakeholder goodwill and avoid public backlash.
7. Manage expectations and maintain credibility.
8. Develop emotional intelligence and understanding of human nature.
9. Balance boldness with caution in strategic decision-making.
10. Surround yourself with strong advisors and foster open communication.

By applying these principles, modern business leaders can navigate the complex landscape of corporate leadership more effectively. Like Machiavelli's ideal prince, they must balance competing demands, make difficult decisions, and maintain their position in a challenging and often unpredictable environment. However, they must do so within the ethical and legal frameworks of modern business, where long-term success is increasingly tied to responsible and sustainable practices.

CHAPTER XI:

The Counsel of Kings: Machiavelli's Advice on Advisors in Modern Business

Machiavelli discusses how a ruler should choose and manage advisors, and how to avoid flatterers. This concept has direct relevance to modern business leadership, particularly in areas of team building, decision-making processes, and organizational culture.

The Importance of Choosing Wise Counselors

Machiavelli emphasized that a prince's choice of advisors is crucial to his success. In the business world, this translates to the importance of building a strong executive team and board of directors.

Consider the case of Apple under Tim Cook. Following Steve Jobs' passing, Cook assembled a diverse executive team with complementary skills. This team includes experts in various areas such as operations, design, and software, allowing Apple to maintain its innovative edge and operational excellence. The diversity of perspectives in Apple's leadership team has been crucial to the company's continued success in the post-Jobs era.

The Danger of Flatterers

Machiavelli warned against surrounding oneself with flatterers, arguing that they prevent a leader from receiving honest advice. In modern business, this relates to the dangers of creating an echo chamber or a culture of yes-men.

The downfall of Theranos provides a stark example of this danger. Elizabeth Holmes, the company's founder, surrounded herself with a board of directors that lacked relevant expertise and failed to provide adequate oversight. The lack of critical voices allowed Holmes to pursue unrealistic goals without proper scrutiny, ultimately leading to the company's collapse.

Encouraging Open Communication

Machiavelli advised princes to encourage their advisors to speak truthfully to them. In the business world, this translates to creating a culture of open communication and psychological safety.

Ed Catmull's leadership at Pixar exemplifies this principle. Catmull instituted the "Braintrust," a group that provides frank, critical feedback on films in progress. This culture of open, honest communication has been crucial to Pixar's consistent production of high-quality films. Catmull's approach demonstrates how leaders can create an environment where difficult truths can be spoken without fear of reprisal.

The Balance of Seeking and Valuing Advice

Machiavelli noted that a wise prince should actively seek advice but should also be able to judge its quality independently. In modern business, this relates to the balance between consultation and decisive leadership.

Jeff Bezos' leadership at Amazon demonstrates this balance. Bezos is known for seeking diverse viewpoints and encouraging debate among his team. However, he's also famous for his ability to make quick, decisive decisions once he has gathered sufficient information. This approach, which Bezos calls "disagree and commit," allows Amazon to move quickly while still benefiting from diverse perspectives.

The Importance of Expertise

Machiavelli advised princes to seek advisors with specific expertise. In the business world, this translates to building teams with diverse skills and experiences.

Microsoft's board of directors provides a good example of this principle in action. The board includes individuals with expertise in areas crucial to Microsoft's business, including technology, finance, and international markets. This diversity of expertise helps ensure that Microsoft's leadership has access to informed perspectives on key strategic issues.

The Role of the Leader in Managing Advisors

Machiavelli stressed that while a prince should seek advice, he must be the one to make final decisions. In modern business, this relates to the CEO's role in managing the executive team and making ultimate decisions.

Alan Mulally's leadership at Ford Motor Company during the 2008 financial crisis illustrates this principle. Mulally encouraged open communication among his executive team, famously instituting a system where executives were expected to raise issues using a color-coded system. However, Mulally was also decisive in making tough decisions, such as mortgaging all of Ford's assets to secure a credit line that helped the company avoid bankruptcy.

The Danger of Inconsistency

Machiavelli warned against constantly changing one's mind based on different advice, arguing it leads to a perception of weakness. In business, this relates to the importance of consistent strategy and communication.

Marissa Mayer's tenure as CEO of Yahoo provides a cautionary tale. Mayer's strategy for turning around the company seemed to shift frequently, from emphasizing mobile to focusing on content to pursuing acquisitions. This lack of consistent direction contributed to Yahoo's continued struggles and eventual sale to Verizon.

The Value of Devil's Advocates

While not explicitly mentioned by Machiavelli, the concept of devil's advocates aligns with his advice to seek honest counsel. In modern business, institutionalizing the role of devil's advocate can help avoid groupthink and encourage critical thinking.

Intel's "constructive confrontation" culture, established by Andy Grove, exemplifies this approach. Grove encouraged employees to challenge ideas regardless of hierarchy, fostering an environment where bad ideas could be weeded out through debate and discussion.

The Importance of Diverse Perspectives

Machiavelli emphasized the value of getting advice from multiple sources. In modern business, this translates to the importance of diversity in leadership teams and decision-making processes.

Satya Nadella's leadership at Microsoft demonstrates this principle. Nadella has emphasized the importance of diverse perspectives in driving innovation and understanding a global customer base. Under his leadership, Microsoft has made significant strides in increasing diversity in its workforce and leadership team.

The Role of External Advisors

While Machiavelli focused on internal advisors, modern business leaders often rely on external consultants as well. The key is to use them wisely without becoming overly dependent.

Apple's relationship with design firm IDEO provides an example of effective use of external advisors. While Apple maintains a strong internal design team, it has collaborated with IDEO on various projects, bringing in fresh perspectives while maintaining control over core design decisions.

Conclusion: The Modern Prince's Council

Machiavelli's insights on managing advisors offer valuable lessons for modern business leaders. The importance of choosing wise counselors, encouraging honest feedback, balancing consultation with decisive action, and avoiding flatterers are as relevant in today's boardrooms as they were in Renaissance courts.

Key takeaways for modern business leaders include:

1. Build a strong, diverse leadership team with complementary skills and experiences.
2. Create a culture of open communication where honest feedback is encouraged and valued.
3. Actively seek advice, but maintain the ability to make independent judgments.
4. Balance consultation with decisive leadership.
5. Avoid creating an echo chamber of yes-men.
6. Encourage constructive disagreement and debate.
7. Maintain consistency in strategy and communication.
8. Value diverse perspectives in decision-making processes.
9. Use external advisors judiciously, without becoming overly dependent on them.

By applying these principles, modern business leaders can create more effective decision-making processes and build stronger, more resilient organizations. Like Machiavelli's ideal prince, they must navigate the complex task of gathering wisdom from others while maintaining their own judgment and authority. In doing so, they can leverage the collective intelligence of their organization while providing the clear direction and decisive leadership necessary for success in the competitive world of modern business.

CHAPTER XII:

Fortune and Virtue: From Medieval Politics to Modern Business

I. Machiavelli's Concept of Fortune and Virtue in Medieval Times

Niccolò Machiavelli introduces two fundamental concepts that he believes shape the success of a ruler: fortune (fortuna) and virtue (virtù). These ideas were revolutionary for their time and continue to resonate in various fields today, including business and leadership.

Fortune, in Machiavelli's view, represents the unpredictable forces of chance and circumstance that can affect a ruler's success. It's the element of luck or fate that can either elevate a leader to great heights or bring them crashing down. Machiavelli likens fortune to a raging river that, when calm, allows for easy navigation, but when flooded, destroys everything in its path.

Virtue, on the other hand, is not the moral quality we

might think of today. For Machiavelli, virtue encompasses a leader's skill, strength, courage, and ability to adapt to changing circumstances. It's the quality that allows a ruler to seize opportunities presented by fortune and to mitigate its negative effects.

Machiavelli argues that while fortune plays a significant role in human affairs, a truly great leader can shape their own destiny through the application of virtue. He famously states that fortune is the arbiter of half our actions, but that it allows us to control the other half.

In medieval times, this concept was particularly relevant. Consider the rise and fall of various noble houses during the turbulent periods of European history. The House of Medici in Florence, for instance, rose to power through a combination of fortunate circumstances (the weakening of rival families) and the virtuous actions of its members (shrewd financial management and political maneuvering).

Another example is the career of Richard Neville, the "Kingmaker" during the Wars of the Roses in England. Neville's ability to switch allegiances at crucial moments demonstrated his understanding of fortune's fickleness and his own virtue in adapting to changing political winds.

Machiavelli advises that a wise leader should be flexible, adapting their approach to the times. When fortune favors bold action, the virtuous leader should strike decisively. When caution is needed, they should be prudent. This adaptability, Machiavelli argues, is key to maintaining power in an ever-changing world.

II. Applying Machiavelli's Principles to Modern Business

While Machiavelli wrote about principalities and rulers, his insights into fortune and virtue are remarkably applicable to the modern business world. Today's business leaders face a rapidly changing environment that would not be unfamiliar to the princes of Renaissance Italy.

1. Fortune in Modern Business

In the business context, fortune can be understood as market conditions, economic cycles, technological disruptions, or any external factors that impact a company's success. Just as Machiavelli's prince had to navigate the tumultuous political landscape of medieval Italy, modern CEOs must guide their companies through volatile markets and unpredictable global events.

For instance, the COVID-19 pandemic represents a prime example of fortune in action. It was an unforeseen event that dramatically altered the business landscape. Some industries, like travel and hospitality, were devastated, while others, such as e-commerce and video conferencing, experienced unprecedented growth.

2. Virtue in Modern Business

In the corporate world, virtue translates to leadership skills, strategic thinking, adaptability, and the ability to make tough decisions. It's the quality that allows business leaders to capitalize on favorable market conditions and to weather downturns.

Modern virtue might include:
- Strategic foresight to anticipate market trends
- Adaptability to pivot business models when necessary
- Resilience in the face of setbacks

- Innovation to create new opportunities
- Emotional intelligence to lead and motivate teams

3. The Interplay of Fortune and Virtue

Just as Machiavelli argued that the most successful rulers were those who could adapt their approach to the times, the most successful business leaders are those who can read the market and adjust their strategies accordingly.

Consider the case of Netflix. The company's transition from DVD rentals to streaming was a perfect example of virtue responding to fortune. Netflix's leadership saw the potential of streaming technology (fortune presenting an opportunity) and had the foresight and courage to pivot their entire business model (virtue in action).

Another example is Apple's introduction of the iPhone. Steve Jobs recognized the potential of smartphone technology (fortune) and combined it with Apple's design expertise and marketing prowess (virtue) to create a product that revolutionized the mobile industry.

III. Concrete Modern-Day Examples

1. Amazon and Jeff Bezos

Jeff Bezos, the founder of Amazon, embodies many of Machiavelli's principles of fortune and virtue. Bezos recognized the potential of e-commerce in the early days of the internet (fortune presenting an opportunity). However, it was his strategic vision, willingness to take risks, and ability to adapt (all aspects of Machiavellian virtue) that turned Amazon from an online bookstore into one of the world's most valuable companies.

Bezos famously said, "I very frequently get the question:

'What's going to change in the next 10 years?' And that is a very interesting question; it's a very common one. I almost never get the question: 'What's not going to change in the next 10 years?' And I submit to you that that second question is actually the more important of the two." This focus on long-term constants amidst changing circumstances is very much in line with Machiavelli's advice to adapt to the times while maintaining a strong foundation.

2. Kodak's Downfall

The story of Kodak serves as a cautionary tale of what happens when a company fails to adapt to changing fortunes. Kodak actually invented the first digital camera in 1975, but the company's leadership failed to recognize the potential of this technology, fearing it would cannibalize their lucrative film business.

This lack of virtue - the inability to adapt and make tough decisions - left Kodak vulnerable when the fortune of the market shifted decisively towards digital photography. By the time Kodak tried to enter the digital market, it was too late, and the company that had once dominated photography filed for bankruptcy in 2012.

3. Tesla and Elon Musk

Elon Musk's leadership of Tesla provides another modern example of Machiavellian principles at work. Musk recognized the growing concern over climate change and the need for sustainable transportation (fortune). He combined this with his own technical expertise and willingness to challenge established industry norms (virtue) to position Tesla at the forefront of the electric vehicle revolution.

Musk's approach also demonstrates the Machiavellian idea of appearing virtuous. Tesla's mission to accelerate the world's transition to sustainable energy has given the company a purpose-driven image that resonates with consumers and investors alike.

4. IBM's Transformation

IBM's transformation under Lou Gerstner in the 1990s is another example of virtue meeting fortune. When Gerstner took over as CEO in 1993, IBM was facing obsolescence as the personal computer revolution undermined its mainframe business. The company's fortune had turned, and it needed a new direction.

Gerstner demonstrated virtue by making the bold decision to shift IBM's focus from hardware to services and consulting. This transformation wasn't easy - it involved significant layoffs and a complete overhaul of the company culture. However, Gerstner's ability to read the market (fortune) and make tough decisions (virtue) ultimately saved IBM and positioned it for future success.

IV. Lessons for Modern Leaders

So, what can today's business leaders learn from Machiavelli's concepts of fortune and virtue?

1. Stay Adaptable: The business world is constantly changing. Leaders must be willing to adapt their strategies and even their entire business models when circumstances demand it.

2. Develop Foresight: While no one can predict the future with certainty, leaders can develop their ability to spot

trends and anticipate changes in their industry.

3. Build Resilience: Fortune will not always be favorable. Leaders need to build organizations that can weather storms and emerge stronger.

4. Seize Opportunities: When fortune presents opportunities, leaders must have the courage and decisiveness to act quickly.

5. Cultivate Multiple Virtues: In today's complex business environment, leaders need a diverse skill set. Technical knowledge, emotional intelligence, strategic thinking, and ethical decision-making are all important virtues.

6. Balance Short-term and Long-term: While adapting to changing circumstances is crucial, leaders must also maintain a long-term vision and build a strong foundation for their organizations.

7. Learn from Failure: Setbacks are inevitable. The most successful leaders, like Machiavelli's ideal prince, learn from their failures and use them as stepping stones to future success.

In conclusion, while the world has changed dramatically since Machiavelli wrote "The Prince," his insights into the roles of fortune and virtue in leadership remain remarkably relevant. By understanding these concepts and applying them in an ethical, modern context, today's business leaders can navigate the complexities of the global marketplace and guide their organizations to success.

The key is to remain flexible and adaptable, to cultivate a range of leadership virtues, and to be ready to seize the opportunities that fortune presents. In doing so, modern leaders can hope to achieve the kind of lasting success that Machiavelli envisioned for his ideal prince.

CHAPTER XIII:

The Call for Unity: From Machiavelli's Italy to Modern Global Business

I. Machiavelli's Vision for Italy

In the final chapter of "The Prince," Niccolò Machiavelli makes an impassioned plea for the unification of Italy. This conclusion is both a departure from the analytical tone of the rest of the book and a revealing insight into Machiavelli's patriotic aspirations.

Machiavelli lived in a time when Italy was fragmented into numerous small states, often at war with each other and vulnerable to foreign powers. He saw this disunity as the root cause of Italy's weakness and susceptibility to invasion by stronger, more cohesive nations like France and Spain.

The author argues that the time is ripe for a new prince to emerge and unite Italy, freeing it from foreign domination. He believes that the Italian people are ready for such a leader and that the circumstances (or "fortune," as he would call it) are favorable for this monumental task.

Machiavelli outlines several reasons why he believes this unification is possible:

1. The Italian people are dissatisfied with their current rulers and eager for change.
2. The small Italian states, while individually weak, have a strong martial tradition that could be harnessed by a unifying leader.
3. The foreign powers that have dominated Italy have shown themselves to be vulnerable.
4. There is a shared cultural and linguistic heritage that could serve as a foundation for unity.

He concludes by calling upon a member of the powerful Medici family, to whom the book is dedicated, to take up this mantle of leadership and fulfill Italy's destiny.

This call for unity and strong leadership in the face of external threats and internal division has resonances that extend far beyond 16th-century Italy.

II. Applying Machiavelli's Call for Unity to Modern Business

While Machiavelli was concerned with political unification, his ideas can be readily applied to the modern business world, particularly in the context of globalization and increasingly complex market environments.

1. The Need for Corporate Unity

Just as Machiavelli saw a fragmented Italy as vulnerable to external threats, modern businesses often find that internal divisions can leave them exposed to competitors and market disruptions. This is particularly true in large, multinational corporations where different divisions or regional offices may operate in silos, failing to share information or work towards common goals.

For example, consider the case of Sears. Once a retail giant, Sears fell into decline partly due to internal conflicts and a lack of unified strategy. The company was divided into competing units that often worked against each other's interests, leading to a fragmented customer experience and inefficient operations.

2. The Call for Visionary Leadership

Machiavelli's call for a prince to unite Italy parallels the modern need for strong, visionary leadership in business. In today's rapidly changing business environment, companies need leaders who can:

- Articulate a compelling vision that unites all parts of the organization
- Navigate complex global markets and geopolitical landscapes
- Make bold decisions in the face of uncertainty
- Inspire and motivate employees across different cultures and geographies

A modern example of such leadership is Satya Nadella at Microsoft. When Nadella became CEO in 2014, Microsoft was struggling with internal divisions and losing ground to competitors in key markets. Nadella articulated a new vision for the company, focusing on cloud computing and artificial intelligence. He also worked to break down silos within the organization and foster a more collaborative culture. As a result, Microsoft has experienced a remarkable turnaround, becoming one of the world's most valuable companies.

3. Harnessing Collective Strength

Machiavelli believed that a united Italy would be stronger than the sum of its parts. Similarly, modern businesses can achieve greater success by effectively combining the strengths of different units or acquisitions.

For instance, when Disney acquired Pixar in 2006, CEO Robert Iger worked to preserve Pixar's unique creative culture while integrating it into the larger Disney organization. This approach allowed Disney to benefit from Pixar's innovative storytelling and animation techniques while providing Pixar with greater resources and distribution capabilities.

4. Responding to External Threats

Just as the Italian states faced threats from foreign powers, modern businesses must contend with disruptive technologies, changing consumer preferences, and global economic shifts. A unified approach is often necessary to effectively respond to these challenges.

Consider how traditional automakers are responding to the threat posed by electric vehicles and autonomous driving technology. Companies like Volkswagen have announced plans to invest billions in electric vehicle development, requiring a unified effort across their traditionally separate brands and divisions.

III. Machiavelli's Principles in the Modern Global Context

Machiavelli's call for Italian unification can also be seen as an early recognition of the benefits of larger, more integrated political and economic units. This idea has clear parallels in the modern world.

1. Economic Unions

The European Union (EU) represents perhaps the most ambitious attempt at regional integration since Machiavelli's time. Like Machiavelli's vision for Italy, the EU aims to create a more powerful and prosperous entity by uniting previously separate states.

The EU has faced many challenges, including the recent departure of the United Kingdom (Brexit), but it has also brought significant benefits to its members, including:

- A large, integrated market that can compete globally
- Increased bargaining power in international trade negotiations
- Shared resources for research and development
- Free movement of goods, services, capital, and people within the union

2. Corporate Mergers and Acquisitions

In the business world, mergers and acquisitions (M&As) often reflect Machiavelli's idea that unity leads to strength. Companies merge or acquire others to:

- Achieve economies of scale
- Enter new markets
- Acquire new technologies or capabilities
- Reduce competition

For example, the merger of Fiat and Chrysler in 2014 created a company better positioned to compete in the global automotive market. The combined entity, now known as Stellantis, benefits from Fiat's strength in Europe and small cars, and Chrysler's presence in the North American market and expertise in larger vehicles.

3. Global Supply Chains

The development of global supply chains represents another manifestation of Machiavelli's unity principle. By integrating suppliers from around the world, companies can:

- Reduce costs
- Access specialized skills and resources
- Increase flexibility and resilience

However, as recent events like the COVID-19 pandemic and trade disputes have shown, global supply chains can also create vulnerabilities. This has led some companies to reconsider their supply chain strategies, potentially moving towards more regionalized models – a reminder that unity, while powerful, must be balanced with resilience and adaptability.

4. Multinational Corporations

The rise of multinational corporations (MNCs) can be seen as a business parallel to Machiavelli's vision of a unified Italy. MNCs operate across national boundaries, often with more economic power than many countries. They face challenges similar to those Machiavelli foresaw for a unified Italy:

- Navigating different cultural and regulatory environments
- Balancing local responsiveness with global integration
- Defending against both local and global competitors

Companies like Unilever and Nestlé have succeeded by developing strategies that allow them to act as unified global entities while also adapting to local markets.

IV. Challenges and Considerations

While Machiavelli's call for unity remains relevant, modern leaders must also consider several challenges:

1. Balancing Unity and Diversity: While unity can bring strength, diversity of thought and approach can drive innovation. Leaders must find ways to unify their organizations without stifling the diversity that can be a source of competitive advantage.

2. Ethical Considerations: Machiavelli is often associated with the idea that "the ends justify the means." Modern leaders must consider the ethical implications of their unifying actions, particularly in a world where corporate social responsibility is increasingly important.

3. Resistance to Change: Unification, whether of countries or companies, often faces resistance from those who benefit from the status quo. Leaders must be prepared to overcome this resistance through persuasion, incentives, or, as a last resort, coercion.

4. Complexity of Modern Systems: The global business environment is far more complex than 16th-century Italy. Leaders must navigate intricate networks of stakeholders, regulations, and technologies.

V. Conclusion: The Enduring Relevance of Machiavelli's Vision

Machiavelli's call for Italian unification, while rooted in the political realities of Renaissance Italy, contains insights that remain relevant in today's global business environment. The core idea – that unity can create strength and provide protection against external threats – continues to drive business strategies, international relations, and economic policy.

However, modern leaders must adapt these ideas to a world that is far more interconnected and complex than Machiavelli could have imagined. The challenge is to create unity while maintaining the flexibility and diversity necessary to thrive in a rapidly changing global environment.

As we navigate the challenges of the 21st century – from climate change to technological disruption to geopolitical tensions – Machiavelli's vision of unity as a source of strength and resilience remains a powerful guiding principle. Whether in business, politics, or international relations, the ability to bring diverse elements together in pursuit of a common goal continues to be a hallmark of effective leadership.

The prince that Machiavelli called for to unite Italy may never have materialized, but his ideas continue to influence leaders who seek to unite organizations, forge alliances, and create entities greater than the sum of their parts. In this sense, "The Prince" remains not just a historical document, but a living guide to the perennial challenges of leadership in a complex and often divided world.

CONCLUSION:

Wielding Machiavelli's Wisdom in the Modern World

As we conclude our exploration of Niccolò Machiavelli's timeless principles and their application to contemporary life, it's clear that the Florentine diplomat's insights remain as relevant today as they were five centuries ago. Throughout this book, we've seen how Machiavelli's teachings can be adapted and applied to a wide range of modern situations, from corporate boardrooms to personal relationships, offering a distinct advantage to those who understand and judiciously employ them.

The enduring power of Machiavelli's ideas lies in their unflinching realism and pragmatism. By stripping away idealistic notions and focusing on the practical realities of power, influence, and human nature, Machiavelli provides us with a toolkit for navigating the complexities of our modern world. Let's recap some of the key advantages that a Machiavellian approach can offer in everyday situations:

1. Strategic Thinking and Decision Making

Machiavelli's emphasis on clear-eyed analysis and strategic planning can significantly enhance our decision-making processes. By adopting his approach of considering all possible outcomes and preparing for various contingencies, we can make more informed choices in both our professional and personal lives. This strategic mindset allows us to anticipate challenges, seize opportunities, and stay ahead of the curve in an ever-changing world.

For instance, in your career, applying Machiavellian strategic thinking might mean constantly assessing the political landscape of your organization, identifying key decision-makers and influencers, and positioning yourself advantageously for future opportunities. It's about playing chess while others are playing checkers.

2. Understanding and Navigating Power Dynamics

One of Machiavelli's greatest contributions is his insightful analysis of power dynamics. By understanding how power is acquired, maintained, and lost, we can more effectively navigate social and professional hierarchies. This knowledge allows us to build alliances, neutralize opponents, and advance our interests more skillfully.

In practical terms, this might manifest as being more attuned to the informal power structures in your workplace, understanding who truly influences decisions regardless of formal titles, and cultivating relationships strategically. It's about recognizing that power often flows through unofficial channels and learning to work within these realities.

3. Adaptability and Resilience

Machiavelli's concept of virtù - the ability to adapt to changing fortunes - is perhaps more relevant now than ever before. In our rapidly evolving world, those who can quickly adjust their strategies and tactics in response to new circumstances will invariably have an edge over those who remain rigid in their approaches.

This adaptability can be a significant advantage in various aspects of life, from adjusting to new technologies in the workplace to navigating changing social norms in personal relationships. It's about being flexible enough to thrive in any environment while maintaining a core sense of purpose and direction.

4. Effective Leadership

While some may find Machiavelli's views on leadership controversial, his insights offer valuable lessons for anyone in a position of authority. His teachings on how to inspire loyalty, make difficult decisions, and balance competing interests can help modern leaders navigate the complex challenges they face.

Whether you're leading a team at work, running a business, or taking charge of a community project, Machiavellian principles can help you lead more effectively. It's about understanding the psychology of those you lead, balancing firmness with fairness, and knowing when to be loved and when to be feared.

5. Pragmatic Ethics

Machiavelli's approach to ethics, while often misunderstood, offers a nuanced perspective on navigating moral dilemmas in a complex world. By understanding that sometimes difficult choices must be made for the greater good, we can develop a more sophisticated ethical framework that goes beyond simplistic notions of right and wrong.

This doesn't mean abandoning our moral principles, but rather developing the ability to make tough decisions when necessary, always with a clear understanding of the potential consequences and trade-offs involved. In a world of increasing ethical complexity, this nuanced approach can be a significant advantage.

6. Personal Empowerment

Perhaps the most significant advantage of embracing Machiavellian principles is the sense of personal empowerment it can provide. By understanding the rules of the game - be it in business, politics, or personal relationships - we can take more control over our own destinies. Machiavelli's teachings encourage us to be proactive rather than reactive, to shape our circumstances rather than be shaped by them.

This empowerment can manifest in various ways: having the confidence to pursuc ambitious goals, the resilience to bounce back from setbacks, and the strategic acumen to turn challenges into opportunities. It's about approaching life with a sense of agency and purpose, rather than feeling at the mercy of external forces.

7. Competitive Edge in Professional Life

In the competitive world of modern business, those who understand and apply Machiavellian principles often find themselves at a distinct advantage. From negotiating deals to climbing the corporate ladder, the ability to think strategically, understand power dynamics, and adapt to changing circumstances can set you apart from your peers.

This doesn't mean engaging in unethical behavior or cutthroat tactics. Rather, it's about being more strategic in your approach, more aware of the underlying dynamics at play, and more skilled at achieving your objectives within the rules of the game.

As we conclude, it's important to remember that Machiavelli's teachings are tools, not moral imperatives. Like any tool, they can be used for constructive or destructive purposes. The key is to apply these principles judiciously, always with a clear understanding of your own ethical boundaries and long-term objectives.

Moreover, it's crucial to balance Machiavellian strategy with other important qualities such as emotional intelligence, empathy, and integrity. The most successful individuals are those who can combine strategic thinking with genuine leadership and interpersonal skills.

In essence, the greatest advantage of understanding Machiavelli is the perspective it provides - a clearer, more realistic view of human nature and the dynamics of power and influence. Armed with this knowledge, you can navigate the complexities of modern life more effectively, make better decisions, and increase your chances of success in whatever endeavors you pursue.

As you move forward from this book, consider how you can apply these principles in your own life. Look for opportunities to think more strategically, to better understand the power dynamics around you, and to adapt more quickly to changing circumstances. Remember that knowledge is power, and the insights you've gained from Machiavelli can be a powerful tool in your personal and professional arsenal.

Ultimately, the true test of Machiavelli's principles lies not in theory, but in practice. As you apply these ideas in your daily life, you may find yourself becoming more effective, more influential, and better equipped to achieve your goals. In a world that often seems chaotic and unpredictable, Machiavelli offers a framework for understanding and navigating the underlying patterns of human behavior and social dynamics.

So go forth with this newfound knowledge. Use it wisely, use it ethically, but most importantly, use it to your advantage. In doing so, you'll be carrying forward a tradition of strategic thinking that has influenced leaders and thinkers for half a millennium. The prince or princess of the modern world is not the one born to power, but the one who understands how to navigate the complex realities of our time. With Machiavelli's wisdom as your guide, you are now better equipped to be that person.

www.ingramcontent.com/pod-product-compliance
Lightning Source LLC
LaVergne TN
LVHW010114170826
845678LV00012B/2406
9781926481180